KNOCK SOMEONE OUT

with ONE punch

By Justyn Billingham

Dedicated to anyone that before reading this book may have had to endure having sand kicked in their face.

You now have the power to turn the tables.

Copyright © 2015 Justyn Billingham

All Rights Reserved. No part of this publication may be reproduced or transmitted in any form or by any means, electronic or mechanical without permission in writing from the author.

Disclaimer
Please note that the author of this book is not responsible in any manner whatsoever for any damage or injury of any kind that may result from practicing, or applying , the principles, ideas, techniques and/or following the instructions/information described in this book. Since the physical activities in this book may be to strenuous in nature for some readers to engage in safely, it is essential that a doctor be consulted before undertaking training.

Contents

Introduction

Basic Punches And More

How To Make A Fist -- Properly

The Fastest Punch Out There

The Most Powerful Punch

The Best Knockout Punch

The Street Fighting Favourite

The Guard Beater

The Hidden Gem

Where do I hit someone?

The Hard Truth

The Elements Of A Successful Punch

Warming Up

Developing Technique

Developing Footwork

Developing Power

Developing Speed

Developing Targeting

Developing Timing

Disclaimer (yes another one)

I'm hoping you're reading this now using that excellent 'Look Inside' feature that Amazon uses as I'd like to have a chat with you about what you can expect to get from this eBook BEFORE parting with your hard earned money.

Plus, given the subject matter I also wanted to explain why I decided to write it.

Firstly let me say that this book was written for anyone that wants to learn *'how to knock someone out with one punch'* for **self defence purposes only**.

Let me repeat that as I think it's quite important.

This book is written for anyone wanting to learn how to knock someone out with one punch in a self defence situation only.

Therefore if your intended use is for any *'other'* purpose I would ask that you **DON'T** buy it. You're not the kind of person I wrote it for.

I also wrote it in order to complement my other top selling book *'Finish a fight in ONE move – without any training'*.

In that book I talk about how to deal with an attack on the street and I felt as great as it is to explain what to do if you're ever come face to face with someone that wants to mug you or hurt you in any way, I also wanted to explain exactly how you knock someone out as I felt that required a whole book in itself.

So that is why this book was written.

In order for you to put into practice the things I talk about in this book you'll need the following.

1. Some kind of bag you can punch (ideally a punch bag) if you plan on training alone. You can pick these up very cheaply these days.

2. A training partner if you don't want to get a punch bag.

3. Some kind of countdown timer. A clock with a second hand or a kitchen style countdown timer will do fine. Or better still a round timer app. There are loads for free on the app stores.

4. If you're training with a partner then you'll need a pair of focus pads. Again you can get these very cheaply now. I'd try to go with new ones as opposed to second hand if you don't know who's had their hands in them before you.

5. A skipping Rope -- optional. You can just jog on the spot.

6. A mirror -- ideally full length but as long as you can see your upper body then this will be fine.

7. A set of focus pads -- or something someone can hold for you to hit.

8. Weighted gloves -- or something you can hold as you punch.

9. A ping pong ball, a piece of string and some tape (or Blu Tack).

Training times table:

Depending on your fitness level I'd suggest the following timings for you.

Beginner (fitness level) -- 60 seconds with 60 seconds rest for FIVE rounds.

Intermediate (fitness level) -- 90 seconds with 45 seconds rest for EIGHT rounds.

Advanced (fitness level) -- 120 seconds with 30 seconds rest for TEN rounds.

And your level is determined by starting at beginner level and seeing how you feel at the end of five rounds.

If you've hardly broken a sweat then move up a level next time.

Introduction

"Touch gloves."

My opponent held out his hand.

I slammed my right fist down on it -- HARD.

Not to try to intimidate him.

But because it was my way of dealing with my nerves.

In a former life I used to be a sales trainer for a mobile phone network.

I always remember being extremely nervous as I'd walk past all the delegates to take my position at the front of the training room and begin the training.

I'd stand there for a few seconds staring back out at the sea of faces that all stared back at me.

I'd then take a deep breath, smile and say in as confident a voice as I could '*Good Morning!*'

The '*duck syndrome*' it's often referred to.

When you see a duck moving gracefully across the top of the water, what you don't see is its legs moving at a hundred miles an hour underneath.

On the surface we can give the impression of being cool, calm and collected just by faking it.

But inside my heart was racing.

So a deep breath, a big smile and a '*Good Morning!*' was my way of dealing with the nerves back then.

And so it was with the slamming of my fist onto my opponent's glove.

That was *'the thing'* I needed to do, just before every fight, to help sort out those nerves.

And don't forget back then (in the early 90's), there was no such thing as the internet.

Or smart phones.

Or Facebook.

So you had a hard time finding anything out about your opponent.

The first you really knew about them was when they stood in front of you.

Thankfully for me he didn't look all that scary.

He didn't have a shaved head.

He wasn't covered in tattoos.

He wasn't pumped up on steroids.

He didn't have any teeth missing.

He just looked like me.

Same size and same build.

I remember pulling up in the car park of a leisure centre once for an interclub event between my Tae Kwon Do school and a rival Tae kwon Do school.

I was around green belt (so about a year training) and walking across the car park in front of our minivan was THAT guy.

Vest top.

Shaved head.

Tattoos.

And I remember turning to my instructor and saying '*he looks pretty tough!*'

To which my instructor rightly replied, '*why, because he has a shaved head?!*'

And sure enough, I ended up facing him on the mats.

And I beat him with relative ease.

He looked the part for sure.

But he couldn't punch his way out of a wet paper bag.

And I remember learning a very important lesson that day.

One that has stayed with me ever since.

"Back to your marks."

We did as instructed.

"You ready?"

My opponent nodded to the ref, still bouncing up and down.

The ref turned to me.

"Are YOU ready?"

I nodded -- also still bouncing.

He stepped back out of the way.

Raised his hand.

"FIGHT!"

My opponent went for it, sprinting towards me, keen to get this over with quickly.

He threw a Jab.

I slipped my head back, raised my left shoulder.

He immediately followed with a cross at exactly the same time as I let off a left hook.

My fist hit something solid.

I chambered my right hand, ready to send a cross, only to see my opponent face plant the canvas.

It was like that moment in Rocky IV when Apollo Creed gets hit with that last punch off Ivan Drago, bounces off the ropes and drops to the floor unable to even put his hands out to stop his face from slamming into the canvas.

My opponent's face hit the ground first.

His legs flicked up behind him.

And then bounced back down again.

I stopped dead.

The crowd erupted.

The ref jumped in between us but there was no need.

It was all over.

One punch.

One incredibly, well timed shot and I had knocked my opponent out cold.

The medics jumped in and began working on him for several minutes but he didn't move.

In the end they had to stretcher him out, shove him in the back of a waiting ambulance and rush him off to hospital.

It was a moment of mixed emotions for me.

I won't lie, I was over the moon about the knockout.

But I was also concerned for the health of my opponent.

Thankfully he made a full recovery.

Yes, anyone can knock someone out.

It doesn't matter how big they are.

Or how small you are.

Yes, there's a technique to it.

But it's not magic.

And it's not out of *your* reach.

And you certainly don't need to join a boxing gym.

Or a martial arts class.

Unless of course you want to.

And you also don't need to spend hours and hours punching away on a heavy bag either.

In order to have a *'Knockout Punch'* you just need to have a couple of simple things in place.

And throughout this book I'm going to teach you what those simple things are.

And then show you how to put them into practice.

So whether it's for competition.

The street.

Ego.

Whatever your motivation is for buying this book.

You too will be able to knock someone out with just one punch.

And lavish in all the confidence that having a 'ONE PUNCH KNOCKOUT' brings.

Basic Punches and More

There are only actually four punches.

A jab.

A cross.

A hook.

And an uppercut.

That's it.

Yes you can find other *'strikes'* contained within all those varying styles of martial art.

Techniques such as:

A backfist strike

A knifehand strike

A palm Strike

An elbow strike.

A hammerfist strike.

An overhand strike.

And they're all great hand techniques.

However there are only actually FOUR main *punches*.

And those four punches are *so* effective that they have served the boxing world more than adequately since John Sholto Douglas, the 9th Marquis of Queensberry first introduced the modern day rules for boxing back in 1867.

And as we all know boxing is a pretty tough fighting art.

In fact its tough and rigorous approach to training (and fighting) uses those four main punches so effective that they can be used to attack at almost any range and at any angle.

And when you combined them with a good understanding of stance, footwork, body mechanics, timing and movement, all four punches can be used with devastating effect.

In fact those four basic punches *are* so effective that you will find a jab, a cross, a hook and an uppercut of some description across pretty much all of the stand up fighting arts today.

So let's get you started on your journey right now....

How To Make A Fist….

… Properly

As daft as it sounds, having taught people how to fight now for the past twenty or so years, it never seizes to amaze me as to the number of people, adults and kids alike, that don't have a clue how to make a proper fist.

So let's start with that.

1. Hold your hand out so that your palm faces the floor with your thumb sticking out to the side.

2. Curl your fingers up and into your palm leaving your thumb still sticking out to the side. And be sure to curl your fingers right up into your palm and not just curl them up into the fleshy bit of skin that sits at the base of the fingers.

3. Bring your thumb in and tuck it under your fingers so it sits just underneath the middle knuckles of your fingers.

Take a look at the photo below to see what you should now be doing.

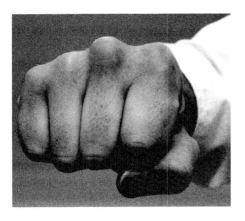

Now here's the thing, you can punch with your fist turned at any angle.

For example, when throwing an uppercut (covered later) you would turn your fist so that your palm faced towards you and the fist travelled upwards towards the ceiling.

Or when throwing a hooking punch (also covered later), it's not out of the question to turn your fist sideways.

What is important in all of this, however, is that you maintain this fist shape at all times.

And here's something else to consider.

There's much debate in the 'martial arts' world as to which are the best parts of the fist to actually strike with.

Some martial arts favour the first two knuckles (the index and middle finger).

Some martial arts favour the last three knuckles (the little finger, the ring finger and the middle finger).

And some martial arts like to use the front (flat part) of the fist and not the knuckles at all.

I personally favour the first option (the index and middle finger knuckles) but that's just me.

The thing to consider when using the last three knuckles is that if you get the punch wrong (and you may well do in the heat of the moment) and attempt to hit with the little finger, ring finger and middle finger knuckles there's a greater risk of you injuring your hand.

You see the little finger knuckle is actually quite weak as it's smaller and sits on the outside of the hand.

So if you catch the target with your little finger knuckle, from experience (although not through personal experience -- thankfully) you'll break your hand.

And that's never a good thing at the best of times let alone if you need to use that hand again to send a second punch.

And as far as using the flat part of your hand (that area between the top set of knuckles and the middle set of knuckles) is concerned, well just try tapping yourself on the head with this area and see how it feels.

Then, using the same amount of pressure, tap yourself on the head with your index finger knuckle and see how different it feels.

The second test, the index finger knuckle test, should have wielded a far greater amount of force on your skull giving way to the fact that the knuckles will do a lot more damage than the flat part at the front of your fist will.

The Fastest Punch Out There

In my opinion the jab is the fastest of all the punches we're going to look at.

It's also one of the simplest to do as well, so a good one for us to start with.

Now here's the thing… you're probably not going to knock someone out with the jab.

It's not really designed for that.

And before you fire up Amazon and give this book a one star negative review (*under a nick name… of course*) hang on in there for just one more minute because I need to explain something.

The jab is a set up punch.

And what I mean by that is as it's thrown off the front hand it's instantly closer to your opponent than your rear hand is, so is therefore *naturally* going to be faster.

And it is.

Whereas the rear hand is further away so will be a tad slower to hit its mark however because it has a little longer to build up momentum and energy, it's a lot more powerful.

So initially you send the jab to stun your opponent.

To get them to react.

Cause them to flinch.

Blink.

Turn their head.

And that's when you send the big rear knockout punch.

At least that's how it generally works.

But first of all *you* need to decide exactly what you want to get from this book.

And what I mean by that is….

1. Do you want to develop a knockout punch for sport?

2. Or do you want to develop a knockout punch for the street?

You're probably going to say *'well both actually'* so let's take a quick second to touch on *'a knockout for sport'*.

If you're planning on facing an equally matched opponent then just *relying* on sending one single punch and hoping it knocks them out is a dangerous tactic.

If that game plan was a guarantee then no one would bother to train for a fight.

We'd all just practice hitting the heavy bag with one single cross punch for an hour and then call it a day.

No, sport is different to the street in a **MASSIVE** way.

It's possible that in the street you may throw one punch and get lucky.

But again, unless your opponent is a complete Muppet, you may *still* need to set up your knockout punch first.

And that doesn't necessarily mean setting it up with the jab first like I mentioned ealrier.

You CAN send just one punch and knock someone out.

I've seen it happen a thousand times.

No, I mean you may have to set up my positioning yourself or your opponent / attacker in the right place.

I feel I may now start waffling off on a completely different track so more information on set ups and ending a street fight in one move have a look at my other book, 'FINISH A FIGHT IN ONE MOVE, *WITHOUT ANY TRAINING*', also available on Amazon.

It focuses on the *complete* street encounter, from awareness, avoidance, engagement, set up and finish.

What it won't do that this book does though is explain *how* to develop a knockout punch.

That's what this book has been written for.

So anyway, back to the jab, and it is an explosively fast, straight moving punch that is thrown off the lead hand.

It is used to judge distance.

To probe through an opponent's defence.

And to set up the more powerful knockout style punch that then follows.

It is also a great long-range technique that has the furthest reach of all the basic punches.

Here's what it looks like at full extension....

And here's how to throw it....

Start by standing in a front facing (boxing style) stance.

You'll note that in this stance the toes point forward.

The rear heel is lifted slightly off the ground.

The legs are just wider than the width of your shoulders.

The rear hand rests on the chin.

The lead hand is held slightly out in front.

The elbows are pulled in close to the body.

This is your basic 'boxing style' front (facing) stance.

Here it is again from a side on view.

From this position 'snap' out your lead hand in a perfectly straight line towards your opponent or target.

Note how the puncher twists his body into the attack.

This is called *'Body Mechanics'* and basically means using your (whole) body to add additional power to the punch.

It's one additional way to get even more power behind an attack with not a great deal more actual effort and massively increase the damage the attack does.

In this instance the puncher turns his complete left (lead) side into the jab.

Follow the foot upwards and see how the punch now comes from the ground, up through the feet, into the legs (that are also *both* turned into the punch) into the hips, into the body and into the shoulders and finally the arm, wrist and fist.

If you can understand this, you're already on your way to massively increasing the power of your punches as most people only really punch using their arm.

Just a couple of things to note, and this is true for all the punches… stay as relaxed as possible.

An arm travelling under tension slows the speed of the punch down and adds more resistance to it which in turn tires you out more.

Now fatigue may not be a problem if you *do* manage to send just one punch and it knocks someone out.

But speed will be of huge importance and tension and resistance will hinder this as well.

So relax.

The only point at which you do tense is at the point of impact.

Once you've hit your target, retract the jab by bringing the hand and arm back again along the exact same straight line.

What a lot of people do is let the arm drop down low as they retract it.

DON'T.

You don't need to.

It's a bad habit to get into.

And it's just plain LAZY.

Plus you also run the risk of your opponent sending a counter attack that you just can't block in time as you're lead hand (guard) is too low.

Out and back on the same straight line!

And don't forget to breathe as you punch.

Either out through the nose.

Or out through the mouth.

It doesn't matter.

Just expel all that energy with the punch.

Imagine doing ten push ups and not breathing.

You'll probably be able to do them but you'll be gasping for breath at the end.

And you'll also run the risk of rupturing something.

Breathe out with every rep (or rather 'punch' in this case).

Now let's look at the first of our knockout punches….

To see the jab in action visit -- https://youtu.be/kQcX0qRoeEg

The Most Powerful Punch

The cross is a great punch and a particular favourite of mine.

As a whole, I think I've stopped more fights with a good solid cross punch than any other.

That said the cross is generally designed to hit straight on so if you have someone standing directly in front of you for example, you would aim to target them on the front of their face.

It travels in a similar way to the jab.

Straight out and straight back in again.

And like the jab it is thrown from a slightly longer range (so you are bit further away from your opponent).

And so if you hit someone with a cross punch straight on there's a possible chance it *won't* knock them out.

And there's a biological reason for this.

How a Knockout occurs
A knockout occurs when the head sustains an impact that causes it to move with such force that the brain, which simply floats around in a liquid atmosphere inside the skull, bounces off the inside of that skull wall causing trauma.

The trauma send a shockwave to the central nervous system which in turns shuts down the brain momentarily giving the body a chance to assess and repair any damage.

Think of it a bit like your household fuse box.

You flick on one to many appliances (like being hit with several punches).

The system overloads (the impact of that final big punch).

And the fuse box shorts out your electricity supply to stop any further damage occurring (your brain, which controls all your conscious motor functions, shuts down).

Now, if you managed to catch someone unawares there's a slight chance their neck and shoulder muscles might just be relaxed enough so that you could get the head to move back with force (translation force) and consequently get a knockout from a straight on cross punch.

However, if they are expecting the blow, or know what they are doing (trained fighter) then there's a good chance they will already be braced for the fight (shoulders shrugged kind of thing) so the impact would be less severe as their neck and shoulder muscles, being naturally quite strong (they have to be in order to hold your heavy old head in place) would absorb a lot more of the damage.

The most effect way of knocking someone out is if you can get their head to whip violently round to the left or to the right (rotational force) as this movement causes much more severe trauma to the brain.

So in order to guarantee (yes, I know you can *never* guarantee something) a knockout, if you can get them to turn their head slightly and *then* hit the chin, this will also cause the head to whip violently to the side (rotational force again) and (possibly) result in a knockout.

And you can either do this by stepping, or zoning out, as you throw the cross punch and hope you're quicker than they are.

Or send that explosively fast jab we just looked at, causing them to flinch and possible even turn their head to the side, thereby opening up the side of their jaw and doing most of the hard work for you.

The cross punch in action (front on view).

In order to send a cross punch your rear hand simply travels out in a perfectly straight line towards the target.

As with the jab, don't just punch with the arm.

Be sure to twist into the punch so that you punch with your *whole* body.

Also, be sure to bring your lead hand back tightly to cover the left hand side of your face against a potential counter strike.

As you'll note from the photo above, the left fist covers the left side of the chin and the right shoulder of the punching arm covers the right side of the chin.

The left elbow and forearm covers the left side of the body and although in the image the right side of the body is exposed, it's only exposed because it's a still photo.

As soon as you have sent the punch, retract your arm back and go straight back into your guard position once more.

In the image below you can see how the puncher has zoned out slightly to the left bringing his body around to the right side of his opponent so that as he sends the cross punch it connects on the right side of his opponent's jaw.

There is a greater chance that this punch would have created a knockout providing it connected with a relative amount of power.

We'll look at how to add power to your punches later but for now let's look at another knockout punch....

To see the cross punch in action visit --https://youtu.be/thjwCyrrjfs

The Best Knockout Punch?

The lead hook is a great, close range punch that is naturally geared towards the knockout.

Any time you watch a full contact fighting event that involves someone getting knocked out when they're standing up, the lead hooking punch often has a big part to play in this.

And the reason this is a great knockout style punch is because of that rotational force thing we looked at in the bit about the cross punch.

As the lead hook connects with your opponents chin, with a decent amount of power, the impact of that connection (often) causes the head to whip violently to the side.

As the neck and shoulder muscles aren't quite as efficient at holding the head in place when the head moves in *this* way as they are when the head moves backwards, it's a lot more likely that the brain will bounce of the inside of the skull wall and cause trauma.

Which is when you get a knockout.

As explained earlier.

And it's also a great punch because it works just as well at close range as it does at medium or long range.

And as a fight / attack can sometime start in either long, medium or close range it's always available to you.

The jab and the cross, for example, don't work quite so well at medium range and don't work at all in close range.

Here's the lead hook in action.

So the key with this punch is the arm position.

As you'll see from the photo the arm is bent, at around ninety degrees -- give or take.

You don't need to get a protractor out at this stage but you get the idea.

And you hook (swing) the punch in towards the target.

Also take note of the position of the fist for a moment.

In the two images the punching fist is turned sideways (so the little finger side of the fist faces towards the floor, and the thumb end of the fist faces towards the ceiling).

The position that you hold your fist in when doing a hooking punch is down to you, however, one thing I will just bring to your attention is the *fist* position in relation to your *wrist*.

Any why this is significant is because of that thing we've all come to hate over time....

Pain!

Ideally as your fist connects while performing a hooking punch you want to keep your fist and wrist in line (straight) as much as possible.

If you hold your fist in the traditional way when doing a hooking punch (palm facing the floor) and the fist connects with a solid target there's a good chance the wrist will buckle causing a sharp pain in the wrist area.

I often find that when working with hooking punches in a class environment, a lot of my less experienced students complain of wrist pain.
Nine times out of ten this is the reason.

So to reduce the chances of your wrist buckling on impact you can do several things.

ONE -- Turn your fist side on.

TWO -- Strap it with a wrist wrap / strap. Just make sure you get someone that knows what they are doing to show you how to wrap your hands and wrists properly (YouTube?) as it's easy to get it wrong and cut off the blood flow to your fist.

THREE -- Always wear a good quality -- and I mean upwards of £20.00, kind of quality bag glove.

Having hit a heavy bag pretty hard for the past thirty years I can't tell you how important it is for you to protect your joints.

Now body mechanics (the movement of the body, remember) were important for the jab and the cross.

But now, they are *really* important.

Now for a moment you need to remember that you're NOT John Wayne (Google him if needed), and this isn't an old cowboy movie you're staring in.

If you swing the hooking punch from your hip like they do in those old John Wayne cowboy movies, particularly against an experienced fighter, that momentary dropping of the fist (your guard) from your chin to your hip could be enough to get YOU knocked out.

So, *don't pull the hand back* in order to build up the momentum.

Or drop it before you punch.

You CAN, and it will certainly give you a bit more power.

But be warned.

It will also slow the punch down and open you up for a possible counter strike.

Instead, keep the fist (your guard) in place.

Twist your body in (towards the target).

And as you do, let the elbow come up from its guard position so the arm is roughly parallel to the floor.

And roughly bent at a ninety degree angle.

And *let your body* do all the work.

This way you can keep your guard in place, throughout the whole of the movement only bringing it away from your face as you literally connect with it.

For longer ranges, do the same thing as above but just extend your arm more in relation to how far away the target is.

Just **NEVER** over stretch or lean too much when you send this punch as you'll no doubt find yourself over balanced and consequently vulnerable.

To see the lead hook in action visit --
https://youtu.be/ljfGM9nXwg0

The Street Fighting Favourite

The rear hooking punch is that punch you regularly see on a Saturday night at throwing out time outside the local pub.

It's the infamous *'throw it from the hip with all your body weight behind it and possible even when your victim isn't looking, let alone prepared'* punch.

Like all those wannabe John Wayne's do.

But that said it *is* an effective punch.

And by effective I mean, if THAT punch (the one I just described above) connects, it's probably going to knock some poor bugger out.

So let's have a look at it and see if we can make it just as effective…

…. Only *much* better.

The principles of the rear hand hooking punch are just the same as they are for the lead hooking punch.

E.g.

You throw it from the chin.

Your elbow bends at approximately ninety degrees.
Your arm travels parallel to the floor.

You use your body to generate the additional power by twisting into it.

Look at the image above.

You'll note that the puncher has zoned out slightly to the right.

A simple step of the right foot will help accomplish this.

However, this on its own, against an experienced fighter will give away what you are about to do.

So for the sake of the explanation, I've isolated this move for you.

But know that you CAN do it as described.

And it might even work for you.

And when practicing the rear hooking punch in isolation, I would advise you to do it like this.

But in reality, it may well be much more effective if sent as a result of a follow up punch, such as a jab.

From the wind up.

Drive the rear hook into the chin of your opponent using your body mechanics (twisting the body).

And then get it back to your guard as quickly as possible, even if you plan on sending out another punch straight away.

Always.

Always!

Get the previous punch back on your chin (guard) first.

To see this punch in action visit --
https://youtu.be/KZF8eDa5Lj4

The guard beater

We're now going to look at our final two knockout punches.

The lead uppercut, as the name suggests, comes off your front hand in the same way as the jab and the lead hook does.

And it is a vertically rising punch designed to target the chin or the body.

And it's a great punch because it's sneaky.

And it's sneaky because of the way it travels -- straight up vertically, which enables it to penetrate through a relatively relaxed or sloppy guard (if a guard is in place at all).

And it's possible that if everything is correct when you send it, you'll get a knockout with it as it will catch your opponent under the chin and cause their head to whip back violently.

So let's look at the lead uppercut in the same way as we did with the lead hook.

We'll isolate it as before and get the body mechanics right.

Look at the image below.

You'll note that the puncher has dipped his lead shoulder.

This is the set up.

As we're isolating this punch for purposes of learning it, to help you get the set up right, just dip your lead shoulder as shown in the image.

However, know that in reality, there's a good chance you'll send this as part of a combination which in turn will mean the previous punch (you throw) will set you up prior to you sending this punch.

As the lead uppercut travels upwards and (when targeting the chin) strikes the underside of the chin, if you can get right underneath the punch you'll be able to use the full movement of your body to increase the energy of the attack.

So dip that lead shoulder and wind up.

Note how the rear shoulder is now in front despite the lead leg still being the predominant one.

Note also how the rear hand (fist) protects the right hand side of the chin and the lead hand (fist) is still firmly on the left hand side of the chin at this stage.

From here drive the lead uppercut upwards aiming to punch up and through the chin of your opponent.

Note (from the image below) how the body twists into the punch as well (body mechanics) to add more energy.

Nothing actually changes from the other punches previous covered so you can see that as long as you get the principles right, all the elements (stance, guard, movement, body mechanics, striking part of the fist etc) are transferable between this punch and all of the punches covered so far.

All that has altered with this punch is that it travels in a different direction to the others.

And as with all these punches, a lead uppercut to the body, in particular the right side of your opponent's body where their liver is situated, is also an incredibly effective area to hit someone.

I once had the privilege of attending a seminar run by one of my all time heroes.

The legendary fighter 'Bill Superfoot Wallace'

If you don't know who he is then Google him.

When I was growing up and just starting out on my martial arts adventure Bill Superfoot Wallace was just retiring from his and in particular was just retiring from full contact, undefeated, competitive fighting and so was a HUGE name in the martial arts world.

And in fact still is.

He had ended an incredible twenty three fight, full contact, kickboxing record, undefeated.

Not only that but thirteen of his wins had been by knockout.

And I got to ask him about those knockouts and his answer surprised me.

I discovered that the vast majority of those thirteen knockouts weren't actually as a result of him hitting someone in the jaw or the face.

The vast majority of those thirteen knockouts were actually as a result of him hitting someone in the body.

The BODY!

He ended a fight by hitting someone in the body.

So when you're considering which punch to use.

What angle to attack at.

Should you use a set up punch or just go straight for the big one?

Keep in the back of your mind that if your opponent's head is well protected.

You punch could be just as effective if aimed at their body.

A knockout punch doesn't necessarily have to knock someone out cold.

It just has to stop them from carrying on fighting.

To see this punch in action visit --
https://youtu.be/DRHlr2_wRY8

The Hidden Gem

This is the last of all the basic punches and it's a good one to end on.

Although the principle for sending the rear uppercut is basically the same as for the lead, due to the fact it comes off the rear hand, and we've established earlier that punches thrown off the rear are more powerful than the lead, this is naturally going to be a much more powerful punch.

Plus, you may well find this punch slightly easier to perform than the lead as you can get into a good position to send it (when isolating it) unlike the lead uppercut that really involves you getting under the punch *before* you send it.

So, let's have a look at this rear uppercut in isolation making sure we use our body mechanics as before and getting right underneath the punch to maximise the energy from our whole body.

From your front facing fighting stance, start dipping your rear shoulder in the same way as you did for the lead uppercut.

Be sure to keep both of your fists (your guard) tight to your chin.

To do this as you dip that shoulder, bring your lead hand (fist) in towards your chin and your lead elbow in towards your body.

You rear hand (fist) should already be in place on your chin.

Then drive your right (rear) hand side directly upwards driving the fist vertically upwards as well aiming to contact with the underside of your opponents chin (if targeting the chin).

As you do, keep that guard tight on the left hand side of your chin and bring yourself back into your original fighting stance as soon as possible.

Naturally if you were planning on sending a further punch from here you would go straight into that but as we're just isolating each punch for now then get in the habit of going straight back into your guard position.

To see this punch in action visit -- https://youtu.be/g2gOYx58T6Y

Where do I hit someone?

So now you know how to actually do each of the punches, we're going to look at how to develop that knockout element by using some very simple training drills.

But before we do that, I want to have another little chat with you.

You see, it's quite possible that you already have a knockout punch, but you may just not know it.

You may be a *'natural'*.

If there is such a thing.

You see it's not so much about technique in all of this, or being a *'natural'* puncher (if there *is* such a thing) but more about knowing *where* to hit someone if you're to stand half a chance of knocking them out.

You see there are TWO main knockout points.

The jaw line.

And the temple.

If you hit someone in either of those two areas there's a greater chance of knocking them out.

The jaw line is a particular favourite as it's a larger target area.

But when you aim for the jaw (*targeting* -- which we're going to look at later) ideally aim for the area of the jaw nearer to the ear.

The reason I say that is because if you aim for the lower area of the jaw and miss, you're probably going to miss altogether.

But if you aim for the higher end of the jaw line and miss, you're more likely to still hit the lower end of the jaw and get the knockout.

I would say that the temple is a secondary knockout point due to the fact that contact with the jaw is going to cause the head to whip round much more than contact to the temple.

But don't discount the temple altogether solely for that reason.

If the jaw's not available for whatever reason, strike the temple.

I had a friend once, back in the days when I used to frequent the occasional nightclub, and this friend formed part of my inner circle of friends so would regularly be on a night out with me.

And as such, he would regularly get himself into a fight.

And I say *fight*.

You see he was slightly smaller in stature.

Below average height.

Some might even say he suffered from that condition we have come to know called '*small man syndrome*'.

Me, I think he just liked a good old scrap.

Now he wasn't necessarily one to start a fight.

But the second....

And I mean the second, anyone outside of our inner circle gave him reason to suspect that they may just have a problem with him.

He'd hit them.

As hard as he could.

On the chin.

There was no skill to it.

He'd just send it off his dominant hand -- John Wayne style, aiming for their face.

And pretty much all of the time he'd catch them off guard, land it and knock them clean out.

Now he never studied any fighting art that may have contributed to this ability.

So in my opinion he just got lucky.

Every time.

And despite what I just said.

Despite me believing he got lucky every time.

In order for him to get that knockout, and not *really* knowing how to throw a punch from a *trained* fighters point of view.

He *was* a natural.

He could naturally throw a punch with all the elements required to knockout someone out, without any prior training.

He just had everything in place.

And that is all that is required for that one punch knockout.

Having all the elements in place.

And that *could* be YOU already.

You *could* already be a 'natural' puncher.

Capable of knocking someone out with one solitary punch.

And how *do* you know if you are a natural puncher?

If you have what it takes to knock someone out with your bare fists?

Well the only way to know for sure would be to find someone.

Punch them in the face as hard as you can.

And see what happens.

Which of course, is highly illegal (unless you feel they are about to attack you -- but that's a whole different thing altogether. Read my other book for more on that).

So on the odd chance that you *aren't* prepared to risk obtaining a criminal record or a short stay in Her Majesty's big house, just to see if you have natural punching ability.

Let's look at a few training drills that will either help you see if you already do have a one punch knockout.

If you are a 'natural'.

And if you're not… well, you will be after this.

The hard truth

Perhaps I should have put this bit at the very start of the book, although I'm hoping that you're the kind of person that appreciates *nothing in life worth achieving comes for free.*

And I don't mean you have to exchange money for it.

I mean you pay in other ways.

Blood, sweat and tears.

Well, possible not the blood.

Or the tears.

But certainly sweat.

And of course your time.

Most certainly your time!

You never get good at anything without investing *'time'*.

From the little life experience I have already had (forty five years of it) I've come to realise there are *two* kinds of people in this world.

The kind that make the world go round.

And the kind that are just happy to go round with it.

The first kind appreciate that in order to achieve anything in life you *have* to put some work in.

The second kind will now be closing this book (*maybe after skimming ahead a little further, just to see if it doesn't actually look like they're going to have to actually do something, then realising they do… and then closing the book).*

The first kind will be firing up the internet and ordering themselves a pair of bag gloves.

The second kind will be firing up the internet and posting a bad review… and then possibly buying another book hoping to find someone out there that will give them that magic secret at how to get good at something without actually having to put any effort in.

I have written several books on the subject of martial arts and fighting.

Have a look for yourself.

One of the books I have written is called '*Kickboxing, from Beginner to Black Belt*'.

In this book I take the lucky reader through the kickboxing journey from white belt through to black belt.

And as kickboxing involves a lot of kicking, naturally there's a section devoted to stretching and leg flexibility.

And as I am somewhat of an authority on the subject (check out the front cover of my book '*How To Develop The Box Splits*' and you'll see what I'm talking about).

So, as that book retails for £16.99 and I figured that stretching is a very important subject, I simply took the chapter on stretching out of it and published it as a standalone ebook -- for sale at just £1.99.

And someone out there bought it.

And then posted a negative review saying '*it was just the same as the chapter in my main book*' (the Kickboxing from Beginner to Black Belt book) that he also owns.

And I had to question why, if he already had EVERYTHING he needed in the first book to help him to develop his flexibility to the point where he too could achieve his dream of a suspended box splits across two platforms like me, did he feel he needed to then buy a *second* book on the **exact same subject**.

And from the same writer.

And the answer my friends, is because he hadn't bothered to follow the instructions in my first book (or maybe he had but simply gave up as he actually needed to work at it a bit) and so thought if he just bought another book on the same subject that one may contain the magic formula we're all searching for.

That 'Get Rich QUICK' style formula.

Or rather, get stretched QUICK!

So let me give you that magic formula right now.

That secret that everyone is looking for.

In order for you to develop all of the elements you need to have in place to ensure that you can hit someone with a single blow and knock them clean out, *you're going to have to actually put a bit of work in.*

It won't come for free.

You pay in time.

With dedication.

With perseverance.

Now remember, I'm not saying you need to go and join a boxing school now.

Or devote thirty years of your life to this like I have.

But you *are* going to need to actually do something.

As simply watching YOU TUBE videos on how to fly a plane doesn't mean that British Airways will come knocking on your door.

And appreciate that I have spent the past thirty years doing most of the hard work for you.

I've made all the mistakes.

I've developed all the injuries.

I've taken all the punches.

I'm now I'm able to impart that worldly wisdom on you.

Share all of my thirty years of experience.

Show *you* the training drills that I spent my whole life doing.

And all for less than the price of a pint beer or glass of wine bought in the place where you may just have to try out those newly developed skills.

So keep this in the back of your mind....

YOU can be the BEST in the world if you want to.

All you need to do to become the best in the world is find the best in the world, at whatever it is you want to do, and simply mirror them.

The elements of a successful punch

To the uninitiated a punch is just a punch.

And that's not a bad thing I guess as it stops things from getting too complicated and blowing our minds.

So you could just leave it there if you wanted.

However, the fact that you've read to this point (and you're still going) tells me you're not about the simple approach.

In order to understand how a knockout punch works so that we can then develop one for ourselves we need to go a little bit deeper and look into what gives a punch knockout capabilities.

And you see, when you dig down deeper you start to discover that a punch is actually so much more than just a punch.

A punch is a single technique made up of several elements that all come together at exactly the right moment to make that punch effective.

Those elements consist of:

Speed
Power
Targeting

And

Timing

And these in turn need to be mixed with....

Footwork

And

Energy – which you will get as you train through all the drills.

So my plan from this point forwards is to show you how you can develop all of the above elements in easy to follow and most importantly, fun drills, that you can do in the comfort of your own home and without the need for you to join an expensive gym or 'fighting school'.

Warming up

Before we go any further, I'm going to tell you to warm yourself up.

If you already train, there's a good chance you already have a good warm up routine so just use that.

If not then here's what I suggest you do, and this is the same warm up routine that I use myself, so I know it's effective.

Skipping

Grab yourself a good rope and start skipping.

Set the timer for five minutes and don't stop (regardless of how badly you skip) until it goes off.

Even if you keep catching the rope on your toes, just reset and start again.

It's a great warm up exercise as it engages large numbers of muscle groups.

It starts the heart beating faster.

And is relatively low impact.

There's loads of ways to skip but if you're new to this then all I want you to do for now is simply bounce from foot to foot keeping up on the balls of your feet at all times.

Try jumping just enough so that the rope just passes under your feet.

It's quite a skill but get good at this and you'll find your co-ordination will improve considerably.

Oh, and choose your rope wisely.

If you stand in the middle of it, the handles should reach up to your arm pits.

If it's any shorter it won't pass over your head properly.

If it's any longer then you can tie a knot in each side (close to the handles) to help reduce the length.

There are also many different types of rope available.

My personal preference is the nylon (speed) type as it's not too heavy but great for speed skipping.

Try a few until you get one you are comfortable with.

If you don't want to skip then just jog on the spot in stead.

Upper Body Rotations

After skipping (or jogging) we'll loosen off the joints.

This will start the *synovial fluid* flowing through your joints (the body's own natural engine oil) and will lubricate those joints of yours and prepare you for all that punching you're about to do.

Circle your arms forward twenty times.

Be sure to take the arms through their full rotation, as shown in the images.

Once you done twenty forwards, do twenty backwards.

Then swing the arms across the front of your chest as shown below.

Be sure to open up your arms fully.

And then hug them tightly across your chest.

That should take you around ten minutes if you do it properly.

Then flick your heels up behind you for sixty seconds.

And then bring them up in front for sixty seconds.

After that, you should be nicely warmed up and ready for the next bit.

Developing Technique

Now here's the thing, let's try and make this as cheap as possible for you.

Don't get me wrong, if you have the money to spend then go mad but why go mad if you don't have to?

The first thing I'm going to suggest you do is find somewhere in your house with a mirror.

A mirror is a fantastic training aid as it doesn't lie to you.

Stand in front of the mirror and simply work your way through each of the punches we've looked out one at a time.

Set yourself a time period of between a minute and two minutes and with good, deliberate movements send the punch out and back again pausing for a second before sending the next one.

As you send each of the punches watch yourself closely.

Look at your feet (if you have a full length mirror -- if not, then just look down).

Do they point forwards (they should) or does your rear foot point to the side (it shouldn't)?

Are your feet evenly spaced either side of an imaginary centre line and are they around shoulder width (they should be) or are your feet close to that same imaginary centre line thereby restricting fluid hip movement from your rear hip and keeping you unbalanced?

Are you twisting your body (body mechanics) as you punch?

Are your elbows in tight to your body or are you giving an opponent an invitation to hit you in the ribs?

Is your rear fist (your guard) tucked in tight to your chin?

Is your lead hand positioned around where your nose is and held out in front?

Are your shoulder shrugged (we call this *Bull Dog neck*)?

These are the things you need to be watching for when you first start developing the technique.

Don't rush through this in a desperate attempt to get to the next training drill.

Take your time and remember, you're building those foundations now.

Your fighting foundations are no different the foundations that your house sits on.

If your house foundations are strong, it will weather any storm and keep you sheltered forever.

If not, it will crumble, and most probably when you need it the most.

Fighting is no different.

I get lots of overly *'keen'* students, normally teenagers, or males in their early twenties that just want to learn that jumping spinning kick they've just seen Jason Statham do in his latest movie.

So I get them to show me their stance.

Their guard.

A simple jab.

And when they can't even do that I suggest we start at the start -- which doesn't always go down well.

It's like, not bothering to learn how to ride a motorbike and instead jumping on the biggest fastest bike you can get your hands on and hitting that throttle.

Weak foundations are a sure fire way of getting yourself into trouble.

Okay, so you've spent several hours in front of that mirror.

You now don't need to look at where your guard is.

Where your feet are.

How your stance is.

Because through all that quality time you've just (properly) invested, you can now *'feel'* if it's right or wrong.

Not only that, but through developing your *'Muscle Memory'* (Google it) in this way, you naturally find yourself in the right position for each punch.

So now let's move on to the next training drill.

Training without a partner

I won't lie, it is going to be difficult for you to develop a knockout punch if you aren't ever able to actually hit something solid.

That said you don't have to spend a lot of money or have your own home gym installed.

If you *do* have somewhere to train at home, such as a garage or spare room, then great but if not, then don't let that put you off.

When I lived with my parents I trained in their garage.

It was full of clutter but I just cleared myself a small space and job done.

My first house that I bought didn't have a garage or a back garden but it did have a side ally so I hung a punchbag on the side of my house and trained outside.

When the dark nights closed in I would set up a desk lamp out there so I could still see.

When the cold weather came in I trained in layers and wore bin bags on my top half (a great training aid to keep heat in and cold out).

And when it rained… well I figured I was going to get sweaty anyway so I didn't care.

And there was something quite cool about being out in the elements training.

You see, people spend more time thinking up reasons why they can't do something, instead of just getting on and doing it.

As I trained on my own most of the time I got myself a punchbag.

When I lived at home with my parents there was no such thing as the internet.

I couldn't drive and the ONLY martial art store that sold punch bags was thirty miles away and there was no way I was lugging a five foot punchbag back home on the train.

So I visited the 'Army & Navy Stores' in my home town, bought myself an army KIT BAG for a fiver (they're shaped like punch bags) and stuffed it full of old clothes.

I then nailed it to the garage wall and there it was… my very first punchbag.

And it did the job fine.

Although as soon as I was able, I got myself a proper punchbag!

And the thing with a punchbag is that it will never let you down.

It's always there for you, ready to train.

And it will give you as much energy back as you give it.

So if you don't have access to a regular training partner, consider packing an old bag with your unworn clothes.

Or get yourself a punchbag.

Then, do exactly the same thing on it as you have been doing in front of the mirror.

And if you have just skipped ahead to this bit to see what else I have planned for you then please don't think, '*sod it, I'll just get the punchbag and forget the mirror thing*' as remember, that mirror is going to help you get your foundations right.

The worst thing you can do is train wrong.

If you train wrong, you'll develop bad habits.

Those bad habits will then stay with you forever.

And if you don't even know you're doing something wrong there's NOTHING you can do about it.

Be your own coach.

You're own best critic!

Get everything right first in front of that mirror.

And then transfer it to the bag.

Training with a partner

If you *do* have the luxury of a training partner then get yourself some focus pads.

Again a small investment but they will last you for ages.

And they can be used for some of the other drills we're going to look at as well.

Let me show you how to work with focus pads to help develop your technique.

Pad held out for a jab.

Ideally the pad needs to be held with the same hand that you are punching off, so if you're punching with your left hand, your partner holds out the left pad.

They also (ideally) need to mirror you so if you stand in a fighting stance with your left leg in front, they need to stand the same way.

Pad held for a cross punch.

Pad held for a lead hook.

Pad held for a rear hook.

Pad held for a lead uppercut.

Pad held for a rear uppercut.

As before, isolate each of the punches and work them for two minutes on the focus pads.

That's all your going to need to do to help you develop your technique.

As you develop your technique you're also going to naturally develop your guard.

Naturally develop your body mechanics.

Your balance.

Your stance.

And your foot positioning.

So can you see how one simple training drill will also develop many others elements.

Next let's have a look at your foot work.

Developing Footwork

Footwork is important as you need to be able to move with grace, ease and agility.

Now don't panic, I'm not going to suggest you start mimicking cats, or tiptoeing through forests without making a sound.

Instead we're just going to go a little deeper and get you moving around now, working all the things you've just been working in the previous section.

If you're training without a partner or equipment I now want you to start shadow boxing.

Shadow boxing simply involves you moving around, sending out random or combinations of punches towards an imaginary opponent.

Imagine you are actually fighting someone.

Move around to mimic how you would follow that person.

See them in your mind's eye and follow them around your training area sending out attacks to their (imaginary) exposed areas (head and body).

Move yourself closer to that (imaginary) person and attack using closer range punches (hooks and uppercuts).

Move yourself back and away from them and attack using longer range punches (jabs and crosses).

As they turn, so do you.

Focus on remaining in your correct stance at all times as you move around.

And try to glide around the floor and not step.

Move forward by just lifting your front foot off the floor just enough and pushing off your back foot.

Remember to stay up on the ball of your rear foot with your heel off the ground.

Move backwards by going light on your rear foot and pushing off your front foot.

The general rule of thumb is to move the leg closest to the direction you want to travel first.

For example, move the forward (front) leg first when moving forward.

Move the backward (rear) leg first when moving backwards.

Move the right leg first when moving to the right.

Move the left leg first when circling round to the left.

This may seem confusing at first and you may just want to just plod around everywhere but resist the temptation to take the easy route as often the easy route isn't always the best route.

Remember this great saying -- **How you train is how you fight**.

Train sloppy and half heartedly and that's how you will fight.

If you don't have a training partner but *do* have a punchbag then do exactly the same.

Try moving around the bag as it swings around you.

Hit it to get it moving and then move around it using your footwork and get in front of it, or behind it, and stop it swinging by hitting it.

Also, don't be afraid to let the bag hit you if you're too close and / or can't get out of the way quick enough as that's also a good way of getting you working your defences.

If you're going to let the bag hit you then don't stop it by simply stretching out your hands.

Stop it by bracing yourself and letting it hit your arms as they cover your body.

Move your arms around so they take the impact of the bag and not your body or head.

Hit the bag from a distance.

Hit the bag from close range.

Hit the bag while moving in close (glide forward).

Hit the back while moving (gliding) backwards.

Hit the bag as it swings around.

Judge your distance from the bag and time (**timing** -- more on this later) your punches so they land perfectly.

Don't hit the bag so you overextend.

Not only will this throw you off balance and open you up, but you also risk injury as you hyperextend your elbows.

Trust me, you'll know when you hyperextend a joint!

If you have a training partner and focus pads then get your partner to move around using their footwork (if they are training with you).

If not, they can just plod around and you follow, gracefully.

As before though, utilise all of the movement we have just covered in the training drills detailed above.

And remember, although this doesn't seem like you're learning to develop a knockout punch as all you probably actually want to do is hit that bag as hard as you can, what you're developing know is footwork and it's footwork that's going to help you maximise the energy you put into the punch.

Think '*wax on, wax off*', and if you've not seen the movie then I urge you to watch it, and the original 'Daniel Larusso' one I mean, not the re-make.

You probably won't appreciate what you're actually doing now until you come to put it all together at the end, so for now let me be your Mr Miyagi and put your trust in me!

Depending on your fitness level I'd suggest the following timings for you.

Beginner (fitness level) – 60 seconds with 60 seconds rest for five rounds.
Intermediate (fitness level) – 90 seconds with 45 seconds rest for eight rounds.
Advanced (fitness level) – 120 seconds with 30 seconds rest for ten rounds.

And your level is determined by starting at beginner level and seeing how you feel at the end of five rounds.

If you've hardly broken a sweat then move up a level next time.

Developing Power

So let's dismiss another popular myth right away.

You don't need to be built like Arnold Schwarzenegger (in his younger, less flabby days) in order to send a punch with enough power to knock someone out.

If that was all that was required then I'm pretty sure Arnie would have been a world champion heavy weight boxer.

In fact the whole boxing world would just be full of body builders or power lifters.

And don't get me wrong, these guys are all powerful guys.

They'd lift the hell out of you and me.

But although power *is* a requirement of a knockout punch it's just one small part it.

I could be the most powerful guy in the world, but if none of those other elements are in place, it makes no difference.

Which is why you don't see many body builders in the fighting world.

And yes it's also true that power comes from the floor, through your feet, into your legs, and across your hips, but you'll develop all of that power through some of the other drills we do.

For now however I want you to develop power in your upper body.

And there's no better method of developing power (through strength) than push ups.

I'm going to give you several different types of push up to try.

My favourite is the good old fashioned *'standard push up'* but you may well find that you prefer a different type, so here are a few more to whet your appetite.

Training Drill One

Wide Arm Push up -- develops power in the chest

Standard Push Up -- power in the chest and triceps

Close Arm Push Up -- power in the triceps and chest

One Arm Push Ups – Isolating muscle groups

Clapping Push Ups -- explosive power

One Arm Medicine Ball Push Ups -- power and endurance

An alternative with this one is to keep the ball where it is but move your body across so you push off the ball with your right hand on the first push up, then the left hand on the second, etc.

Medicine Ball Push Ups -- power and stabilising

Decline Push Ups -- Power in the upper chest and shoulders

The '*one arm medicine ball*' push up and the '*Swiss ball*' push up can also be varied using the different hand positions from the other push up drills in order to work different muscle groups.

My suggestion for all of the above exercises would be to add variety to your workouts by working a different style of push up each time.

Start off with the wide arm push up for example and working through to the Swiss ball push ups.

Alternatively you could choose to take several (I would suggest no more than three) of the push up drills above and use those as part of an overall upper body power development training programme.

Whatever you do, be sure you are fully warmed up first before you do it, and then take each one to failure (so do as many as you can without stopping before you can't do another one).

Ideally when you do each push up, slow it down.

It should take you two seconds to lower (make sure your nose and chest touches the floor) and two seconds to raise yourself back up again (straight arms).

If not, then you're just using momentum which won't work the muscle properly.

Plus, it's called 'cheating'.

Make a note of the number of push ups you achieved, allow yourself a few days rest to give the muscles chance to recover, and aim to beat that number the next time you do it.

Training Drill Two

Weighted Gloves
Weight training is a great way to develop power in your punches but you don't need to sign yourself up to a Virgin Active Gym in order to develop a knockout punch.

Just adding a bit of resistance will get the muscles working harder which in turn will make them stronger.

My suggestion would be to get yourself some weighted gloves.

Then be sure you to stick to these strict guidelines:

Guideline One -- Use gloves that allow you to adjust the level of weight. Most weighted gloves have small sandbags in them that you can add and remove. Avoid ones with a fixed weight that could be either too heavy or too light in the beginning.

Guideline Two -- **NEVER** punch at full speed while wearing weighted gloves. This is a sure fire way to injury.

Guideline Three -- **NEVER** punch a target wearing weighted gloves. Only punch the air (*at a reduced speed* -- see *Guideline Two* above).

My suggestion is to use them now as part of your *shadow sparring session* -- use the same timings as suggested at the start of the book.

If you don't have access to weighted gloves then you *can* substitute them for light hand weights or a similar, easy to hold, weighted object.

Just don't drop it on your toe.

Developing Speed

Quite simply, you want to throw that punch so fast that your opponent doesn't even see it coming.

If they don't see it, they can't stop it.

With a little bit of training here, we'll increase your punching speed to a point where, even if they *do* see it coming, it will *still* be so fast they won't be able to do anything about it.

A bit like a car crash.

You see the idiot pull out in front of you, but it all happens so fast there's nothing you can do about it.

Now, the type of speed we need here is *explosive* speed and there's a difference.

If you threw fifty punches in thirty seconds it would be fair to say you could throw a lot of fast punches.

That, however, is not what we want.

We need to be able to go from stationary to landing it without your opponent being able to do anything about it.

That's explosive speed.

We're not going to throw fifty punches at our opponent because we're not in a Karate Kid style competition where it's all about landing as many punches as you can in a given time period and the fighter that lands the most punches in that time period wins… on points.

We're planning on sending just ONE punch and knocking someone out with it.

So here are a few simple (and fun) drills to help you develop that kind of speed.

Training Drill One

Beat your partner
This is a great drill for helping you develop explosive speed, but you do need a training partner for this to work.

You need to hit the target / pad with a punch before your partner can move the pad out of the way.

The pad feeder can't move the pad until you move (to hit it).

Make it even more fun by being the first person to score ten (ten hits or ten misses) and add a forfeit in for the loser.

Training Drill Two

Hand slap
This time your need to hit the pad and retract your hand before your partner can slap it.

Add some competition in to this by doing ten attacks and then switch around so that your partner tries to beat your score.

Training Drill Three

Broken rhythm

This time the pad feeder starts with the pads on their chest.

As they present a pad, the puncher attempts to hit the pad as fast as they can with the correct technique, based on how the pad is held.

The pad feeder then places the pad back on their chest and using broken rhythm presents the next one.

Training Drill Four

Reaction time

As above but this time the pad feeder names the technique as they move the pad into place.

The puncher needs to react as fast as possible, striking the pad with the correct technique.

Add an element of competition to this by only holding the pad in place for a few seconds before bringing it back to the chest again.

Developing Targeting

You can be the most powerful puncher in the world, with the most explosive of punches, but none of this matters if you miss your target every time you throw a punch.

I've been studying the fighting arts as well as teaching people how to fight now for over thirty years and in that time one thing has become apparent... people don't really know what they should be doing.

And what I mean by that is that I regularly see students randomly throwing out attacks that wouldn't land in a million years, just because they are 'sparring', and just because they think that's what they should be doing.

They think they *should* be attacking so better to just attack than not.

And all they manage to do is miss their target, tire themselves out and open themselves up for a counter strike.

Or worse, just bounce every attack off their opponent's nice tight guard.

And then just keep on doing it.

If instead they just reduced the number of attacks they threw and made sure that every attack they did throw was on target, most of them would dramatically improve their ability to fight.

Plus, they wouldn't be so worn out at the end.

So think of it like this.

Fifty, full power, explosive *wasted* punches are of no use to anyone.

One, full power, explosive, *targeted* shot is worth everything.

A good friend of mine and former world kickboxing champion (several times) proved this point once while fighting a very highly skilled opponent that wanted his title.

In the first round of their fight he allowed his opponent to unload all of his attacks on him while he simply covered up or moved out of the way of them.

The first round passed and he hadn't thrown one technique.

His opponent had thrown hundreds.

The second round passed and he still chose not to throw a punch.

His opponent threw hundreds.

We all thought for sure he was going to lose on points if he carried on.

His coach (his father) was screaming at him throughout.

But he stayed cool, calm and collected and waited patiently for the perfect moment.

When that perfect moment presented itself he hit his opponent with one single rear uppercut that was so fast, so powerful and so well timed it lifted his opponent off the floor, like in a scene from a Rocky movie, and sparked him out cold before his head even hit the canvass.

After we asked him what he was thinking and his reply....

'I just wanted to see if I could land the perfect punch.'

He certainly did that.

His punch was timed incredibly.

He targeted the chin of his opponent with laser guided accuracy.

It was so explosively fast none of us saw it, let alone his opponent.

And it was so powerful it knocked his opponent out cold.

One punch and he didn't even break a sweat.

Here are a few drills to help you develop your targeting to that level.

Training Drill One

Ping Pong training
This training drill can be done alone, is incredibly inexpensive and amazingly effective.

Attach a piece of string to a ping pong ball with sticky tape or blu tack and hang it from the ceiling at around head height.

Then move around as if you were sparring aiming to hit it each time you send a punch.

Start off by isolating one punch, the jab for example, and then change the punch.

Then move around sending all of your punches as if you were hitting a punchbag.

As you hit the ping pong ball make sure you are hitting with the correct part of your hand (the knuckles).

Training Drill Two

Pad throw
This drill can be quite a fun one, just be sure you have plenty of room to practice with nothing breakable in the near vicinity.

Simply throw a focus pad (or target) into the air.

And attempt to strike it with your chosen punch before it hits the ground.

Training Drill Three

Spin drill
This is another fun one but with a serious side attached to it as well.

Quickly spin round ten times taking care not to fall over -- you might need help with this one.

Then strike the target with a chosen punch or punches aiming to hit as accurately as possible with each punch.

You can either punch a punch bag, the ping pong ball (which will be harder as it will move so you'll have to track it) or focus pads.

Little note -- The effects of spinning around like this is the closest you'll get to the feeling of being dazed as a result of getting punched on the chin or temple without actually having to get punched.

If you can control the head spin and still target your shots then you have a good chance of recovering from such an attack.

Not only that but it is a fun drill to try.

Developing Timing

Timing and speed (or rather, speed and timing as it's generally referred to) go hand in hand together.

You could be the fastest puncher in the world, but if your timing's rubbish, then all those lightning fast punches will simply miss, or bounce harmlessly off the guard of your opponent.

So what is timing?

Good question!

Timing is the ability to send a punch at exactly the right moment so that the chances of it landing are greatly increased.

The advantage here is obvious.

Timing is also used in defence.

A fighter will wait for their opponent to attack, blocking or evade, and return with an attack of their own.

A well timed counter attack has a greater chance of landing.

So let's look at how you can develop incredible timing that, when combined with explosive speed, will ensure your attacks are unstoppable.

Training Drill One

Hand slap
Face your partner.

Your challenge here is to slap your partner on the hand before they can touch you on the chest.

If your partner has been training the *'speed'* drills with you then this will make it all the more competitive, so your timing here will need to be really good.

Plus this drill will also help whoever does the chest touch, to further develop their explosive speed.

Make it more competitive by adding in a forfeit.

This time, *you* decide what the forfeits are for.

Training Drill Two

Parry, Attack

Face your partner.

Get them to throw a jab towards your face.

Knock the jab off target (this is called a 'Parry') with the hand you're *not* going to punch with (so you use your timing to 'parry' their attack).

And immediately send back a jab as a counter.

Change the punch you use to attack with each round.

Training Drill Three

Leg jump
This timing drill is great fun but does require a great deal of trust.

Start in position one (below).

Jump into the air as high as possible while your partner opens their legs.

And land in the centre.

As soon as you touchdown, spring back up again, as your partner closes their legs, and land back into the start position

Continue jumping and opening / closing the legs for a set time period based on our fitness level (refer to the *training times* table at the start of the book).

Training Drill Four

Pad throw (from earlier)
This drill can be quite a fun one, just be sure you have plenty of room to practice with nothing breakable in the near vicinity.

Simply throw a focus pad (or target) into the air.

And attempt to strike it with your chosen punch before it hits the ground.

In Summary

I wanted to keep this book as simple as possible.

Not because I wanted to write as little as possible but because I wanted to you to be able to get the best out of it.

You see, over my time I have trained with some amazing people, learnt from the best in the world, read hundreds of books on training, fighting and martial arts and watched hours and hours of video footage on the same subjects and the one thing I have come to realise is -- *you have got to keep it simple.*

Everyone has their own unique ways of doing things and most of the time when they are asking you to give them money for showing you them, they feel they want to give you your money's worth.

At least that's how it should be.

And I'm no different.

However, in giving you loads and loads of information, there's a danger of making things *too* complicated.

For example, there are many different points on the human body that you can attack.

And there are many different techniques that you can attack with.

But if I give you twenty different areas of attack combined with a unique way of hitting each of those twenty areas, and then you have to one day use any of that information for real (God forbid), there's a massive risk you'll suffer from something called '*information overload*' which basically occurs when there's too much to think about… and you freeze.

Plus, I could also give you hundreds and hundreds of training drills to do because there's hundreds out there -- but there's no need.

Instead I have given you what I would consider to be everything you actually need in order to achieve your ultimate goal of developing a knockout punch.

I like to call it '*Minimum effort for Maximum results*'.

The minimum amount of work that you have to do in order to achieve whatever it is that you want to achieve.

If you want to make a cup of tea you put a tea bag in your mug, boil the kettle and pour the boiling water in the mug.

Job done.

What you don't do is boil the kettle, then pour the boiling water into a saucepan and continue heating it on the stove, and then pour it into a measuring jug and heat it in the microwave -- just to be on the safe side.

Boiled is boiled -- you can't boil something more.

But endlessly training different types of drills in order to achieve the same end result is the same thing as the above example.

Google 'Mike Mentzer' to see what I'm talking about.

Doing twenty different drills on how to develop speed is pointless.

You just need to super develop one until you're as fast as you can be.

Because once you have got as fast as you can be, you're not going to get any faster.

I hope that makes sense.

You don't need to know the ins and outs of how a mobile phone works in order to make a phone call.

Admittedly I've gone deep on a few subjects but I went deep when I saw a need.

If it's not going to benefit you in any way, I left it out.

The key thing for developing any skill is repetition, repetition, repetition of that one skill.

The only reason all those health and fitness magazines come up with new and innovative ways of building muscle each month is to simply get you to buy the magazine.

You wouldn't buy it if they just printed the same thing over and over again.

But it's those tried and tested, old school training methods that work (have you not watched a Rocky movie? -- just joking but do you get what I'm trying to say?).

If you want to build a big chest then do bench press on a weights bench.

Don't waste your time doing bench press on a Swiss ball with chains instead of weight plates, regardless of what the magazine says about it.

Do you see what I'm getting at?

There are hundreds of drills out there for developing speed.

I've chosen the ones I think work best for what you need.

They worked for me all my training life and I could hit you so fast you wouldn't see it coming -- trust me.

But don't forget in all of this that developing a one punch knockout is completely different to learning to spar.

Or training to become a great fighter.

That's something completely different and for that you will need someone to train you.

You can't learn that from a book.

But if all you want to be able to do is hit someone that chooses to attack you, with one sold punch that catches them in exactly the right spot and is sent with enough speed and power to knock them out cold….

… Well, then you have that in this book.

Final Word

So there you have it.

Everything you need to help you develop that knockout punch.

Whether you actually go on to develop a knockout punch now entirely is up to you.

I used to spend a lot of my time desperately trying to encourage people that I saw potential in to *better themselves*.

I'd give up precious family time to head round to someone's house and spend the evening telling them what great potential I saw in them.

And you know what, not one of those people ever bothered to do anything about it.

And for quite some time I struggled with this.

I struggled to understand why, when someone had huge potential, did they choose to do nothing with it.

When someone could go on to achieve incredible things with their life, did they choose not to.

Until one day it dawned on me.

You have got to want to do it for yourself.

Yes, it's great to have someone tell you that you could achieve incredible things but unless you have that special *something* inside that gets you up and off the sofa and springs you in to action, it's just words falling on deaf ears.

So what kind of person are you then?

Are you the kind of person that helps make the world go round?

Or the kind of person that is just happy to go round with it?

You now have the power to achieve something incredible.

Develop a knockout punch.

How many people do you know that can knockout someone out with one single punch?

It's like getting your first Black Belt.

How many of your friends have a black belt in a martial art?

And I want you to understand now that this book can be so much more than simply a way for you to develop a knockout punch.

But none of that is for free.

In order for you to develop a knockout punch you are actually going to have to drag yourself away from that TV and do something.

And to be honest with you, *that* is probably going to be the hardest thing for you.

NOT the training.

Getting going may not even be that hard.

You're currently entering into the fun stage, also known as the *'honeymoon period'* when it's all fun and new and exciting.

The challenge is going to be when that all wears off.

When you get a little bored.

A little de-motivated.

Because you'll quit.

So my advice is **DON'T**.

Keep going when you hit that wall -- and it *will* come.

Push yourself through all the challenges you'll face.

When you get back home tired from a tough day at work or school and just want to collapse on the sofa -- GO AND TRAIN.

Trust me, you'll feel so much better for it.

When I was fourteen years old I was a complete failure.

The product of a broken home.

A one parent family.

I was destined to be another of life's losers.

And then something quite horrific happened to me that changed my life.

I got viciously attacked one day by a couple of youths and ended up in hospital.

As a result of that one event I got the motivation I needed to go and study the fighting arts.
My mother couldn't afford to pay for my training so I got a job washing pots and pans in a busy pub kitchen so I could pay my own way.

While all my teenage friends were out having fun on a Friday and Saturday night, I was stuck in a hot sweaty kitchen washing up.

And I hated it.

I hated the job and I hated the discipline of the training.

I was a fat, lazy kid that just wanted to sit in front of the sofa and eat.

But the fear of being attacked again motivated me to stick with it all.

And I'm so glad I did because as a result of forcing myself to do something I didn't want to do (in order to better myself), thirty years later I now live the life I want to live.

I drive my dream car.

I do the job I want to do (and I love it).

And I get to spend time with people that I love to be around.

I won't bore you with all the details, needless to say that I could have taken the easy way out so many times.

But I didn't.

And I'm not telling you this to try to impress you.

I'm telling you this because I want YOU to achieve whatever it is you want to achieve in life.

Most people NEVER achieve their dreams.

They reach their deathbed with regrets.

Before I started studying the fighting arts I was the last kid to get picked for any sports team.

I was in the bottom class for most school subjects.

I really couldn't be bothered.

But when I finally managed to achieve my very first black belt I realised then and there that I could achieve anything I wanted to.

All I had to do was to apply myself in the same way that I had done in order to achieve my black belt.

And so I did.

It was that one final moment of realisation that finally changed my life.

So don't just put this book down now and promise yourself that you'll start next week.

Because you won't.

And don't go and buy another book on the same subject looking for some magic secret because you have that magic secret in this book.

Just promise yourself, like I did, that you're going to see this through.

Because who knows where that attitude will take you?

Where you may just end up?

And please keep in touch -- justyn@blazemartialarts.com.

You may have some questions?

But most of all I'd love to hear from you.

Good luck and future success,

Justyn

Printed in Great Britain
by Amazon